# THE
# *Beer*
## BOOK

Printed in Japan.

International Standard Book Number: 0-8256-3236-6
Library of Congress Catalog Card Number: 81-52582

In Great Britain:
Book Sales Ltd.
78 Newman Street
London W1P 3LA

In Canada:
Gage Trade Publishing, P.O. Box 5000,
164 Commander Blvd.
Agincourt, Ontario M1S 3C7

Cover design by: W.D. Jurgeleit

Cover photographs by: Isabelle Francais
Photo on page 57 appears through the courtesy of Miller
Brewing Company.

# Contents

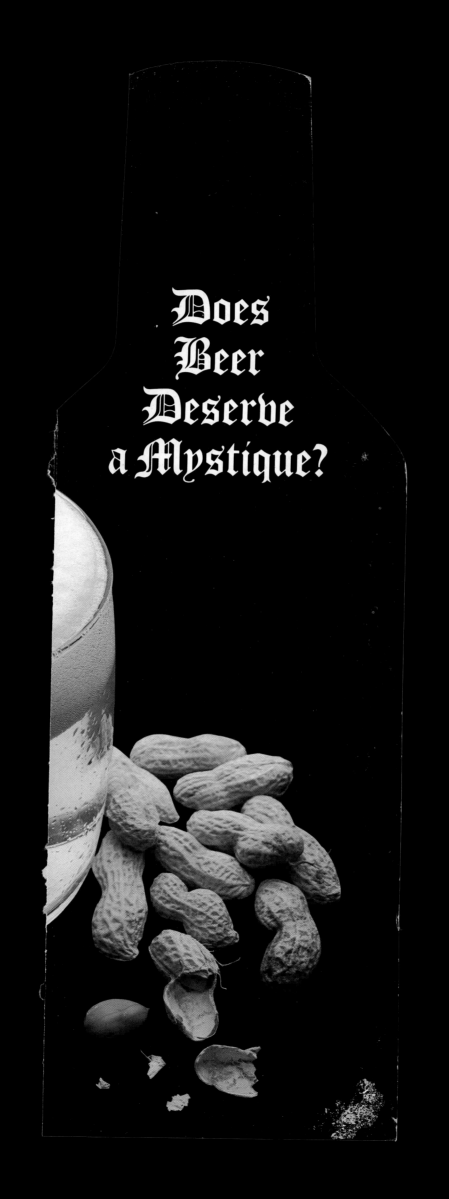

# Does Beer Deserve a Mystique?

The news that Samuel Smith's Old Brewery Pale Ale is "Supreme Champion" of British beerdom was not regarded as news in North America. News about beer is seldom news in America, unless it's a business story. The news that Coors is going to produce a super-premium beer—rather exotically called George Killian's Irish Red Ale—received scant attention. The days are gone when Coors could choose its distributorships as though awarding knighthoods, doling out its modish beer to a marketplace that seemingly could not get enough of it. The threatened demise of the Pittsburgh Brewing Company, as a result of labor troubles, was news because it would have meant yet another brewer had failed to survive in this highly competitive industry. Moreover, the 120-year-old company was the city's last remaining brewery.

Yet to a beer-lover, these events hold different meanings. That Samuel Smith was ranked first among seventy of England's best brews competing at the Great Western Beer Festival in Bristol was especially good news—good news for the 222-year-old Tadcaster, Yorkshire, brewery as well as for many Americans because this exemplary ale is being exported to the United States. By contrast, the news from Coors was at best intriguing. Many beer drinkers find Coors Banquet Beer much too light and wonder whether the so-called mystique about the beer wasn't based almost entirely on its relative exclusivity. Coors, which is now building a plant on the East Coast, used to be available only in a limited number of states in the West and Southwest. What the beer-lover is primarily interested in, therefore, is what's this new beer going to taste like? How will it compare to Michelob, to Erlanger, to Andecker, to other super premiums? Perhaps more germane, how will it taste compared to the Biere Rousse made by

6

# Does Beer Deserve a Mystique?

Pelforth of France, on which the Coors beer is modeled, which itself is made under license from George Killian Lett of Enniscorthy, County Wexford, Ireland. Lett no longer brews his ale, but he has licensed not only the rights to it in Pelforth, but a delicious little legend as well: While astride his horse one day, Ireland's first king found himself enveloped in a magic cloud, wherein he met a Celtic god. Accompanying this deity was a beautiful young maiden, symbol of Ireland's sovereign status. In order to pay proper homage to the occasion, she gave the king a glass of foaming red ale. Since the very knowledgeable Michael Jackson, English beer authority, has described the Pelforth descendant of this godlike brew as "full-bodied, copper-coloured ale, malty without being unduly sweet, and with a strong, smooth taste," that ancient king must have felt himself a very lucky sovereign. And Americans will consider themselves lucky, too, if the version from Coors honors the legacy of this beatific brew.

If Coors can merit a mystique, so, surely, does beer as a worldwide entity. It is consumed on a worldwide basis, and has been since the dawn of civilization. Its history is as rich in events and its legends as rich in fervor and imagination as those emanating from any other alcoholic beverage. And among the thousands of brands around the globe are many brilliant representatives of the brewer's art. Fit for kings—very grand stuff. Just ask that first king of Ireland. . . .

# A
# Romance
# with
# Beer

# A Romance with Beer

crank of my acquaintance—namely the editor of this book—recently shared with me a smattering of his vast knowledge of the world. Beer, he beamed in my direction, was the third most popular beverage in the world. Despite the fact that I realized he was merely displaying—and doubtless exhausting—his knowledge of the subject, I felt obliged to dissuade him of this notion.

Beer, you see, is *not* the third most popular beverage on this planet. It is, in fact, second only to tea, which is a more popular beverage only because of the ingrained drinking habits of millions of Asians and a relative handful of island-bound Britons who believe that drinking tea will somehow improve the weather. Not that I disapprove of this notion. It's just that I happen to know that British beer is more of a palliative in this instance. And anyone who regards water as a beverage is mucking up the sacrosanct order of things in the universe.

Among alcoholic beverages, it's first beer, then wine. This is another indication of the priority of things.

If I sound fairly militant about these matters, it is because I have had to travel a hard road from non-discriminatory imbiber of beer to genteel quaffer to registered beerologist. For example, when I was a lad in college, the obligatory thing to do of an evening was to head for the nearest beer emporium. Massing in groups rivaling the size of football squads, we'd consume—indeed, guzzle—as many pitchers of beer as our collective bladders and budgets could withstand, and talk of manly things. Mostly sports, girls and sex, and generally in that order since few of us were truly conversant with the inner workings of coeds. Thus, whenever it seemed appropriate to reveal the inner workings of our sex lives, we'd instead

10

# A Romance with Beer

break out into song—usually drinking chanties of a low order—and indulge in chug-a-lugging contests.

I will concede that it didn't really matter to most young American lads of a certain class, period and ignorance, that the beer they consumed so avidly was fairly often of a discernibly vile nature. It was cheap. It generally tasted palatable after your taste buds were sufficiently anesthetized. And even if it *never* tasted good, it inevitably made you feel good. Perhaps that's why hedonism is always wasted on the young. They have no taste.

In truth, I don't recall ever appreciating a beer strictly for its taste qualities while I was a university student. Oh, American beers could be refreshing—and who should ask for anything more! It wasn't until I was in the army, stationed in a small town in Germany, that I came to understand that beer was not merely a refreshing (and reliably mood-elevating) beverage, but also very tasty. Indeed, a noble brew. Thus began my love affair with beer. Ansbach, Germany, was the site, a town of 30,000 men, women and farm animals, distinguished by a Bach festival in the summer and four breweries providing twelve superior brands of Bavarian-style beer all year long. Plus bock in the spring and dark,

# A Romance with Beer

super-rich beers during *Oktoberfest* and *Fasching*. This was heady stuff for a kid from Connecticut.

I traveled widely in Europe and I learned a little something about the wine culture throughout the south, and about the beer culture throughout the northern European nations. In Denmark, northern Germany and the Low Countries, northern France as well as Alsace-Lorraine, where the language is French but the beer style German, I found an enduring romance with beer that was absolutely unduplicated in America. Not that Americans didn't drink beer; they didn't esteem it as they do in Europe. America had no beer culture.

Since those early days of flowering sensibilities, I have been fortunate enough to log a good deal of time—usually as a working journalist not only in Europe, but in Ireland and the British Isles as well—and I yield to no Englander or Scot or Irishman in my affection for man's noblest institution, the pub. Some are charming and some are of considerable architectural interest and some are pretty grubby, but if the beer is flavorful and there is someone to join in good talk, I find them places to warm the heart and make clichés come true. And to admire the romance of beer in perhaps its fullest flowing.

When in London, I find myself gravitating less and less to "tied houses" owned by the national brewers, however atmospheric, and instead seeking out pubs owned by the smaller local brewers—Young's and Fuller's in particular—or else wonderfully eccentric emporiums of taste such as the late, very much lamented Becky's Dive Bar. No frills here—you could get your feet wet going to the men's room because this Thames-side pub was once the site of a debtors' prison—but Mrs. Rebecca Willeter stocked "two hundred lovely

# A
# Romance
# with
# Beer

# A
# Romance
# with
# Beer

beers,'' as she was wont to describe them. Ruddles and Dutton's of Blackburn and Warwick Stout and Benskin Colne Spring and Dublin Guinness—not the London brew—was what Becky's was all about.

My current favorite London pub is the Sun Inn on Lamb's Conduit Street. A small place with no architectural distinction whatsoever. But the publican not only brews his own excellent Berman 6X, but offers twenty-three real ales. In addition to such splendid brews as Brakspear's and Theakston's and Greene King and the Welsh Felinfoel, there are weekly specials from around England. When I last visited there with one of Earth's most serious beer tasters, Mr. Richard Gilbert, deputy editor of *The Listener,* the BBC's weekly magazine, he was as dazzled as I was by the blackboard selections: ''Hydes/Hartleys/Pollards/ Taylors/Jennings/Simons.'' As eminent grammarians, we wondered if there might not be an apostrophe or two missing from this list, but after two hours of liquid research our only grumble was with England's inhumane pub licensing hours.

In Scotland, there does not exist this wide choice of excellent beers, but you *do* find a few world-class ales. Although I've experienced a smidgen of Welsh partisanship on the question of ''best beers,'' the Welsh usually stand quietly by, never playing at being Dylan Thomas. But they are very serious about their beer, although I haven't found them anywhere as vocal about it as the Scots. While it is not world knowledge, the Scots are probably as proud of their brews made from barley as they are of their whiskies made from the same source.

Yes, in Scotland there is much ferment in barley. One evening, while enjoying the facilities of the ''island bar'' of the Abbotsford, a lovely old pub on Edinburgh's

# A Romance with Beer

Rose Street, I committed the diplomatic error of speaking well of brews made south of the border. Meant as a gesture of good fellowship, it was received in the manner of a gauntlet thrown in the face of Robert the Bruce. Ha, Scottish ales are stronger, worthier and in all respects the only ales about which a serious drinking man should froth off at the mouth about! In sheer self-defense, I counterattacked with Newcastle Brown Ale, which is damn strong, unique and just happens to be made by a Scottish brewer. And promptly bought a round of same. They then hit at my flanks with Younger's Double Century Ale. I fought back with reinforcements from Newcastle. They tried to overwhelm me with both MacEwan's and Tennent's, but I kept calling up still more reserves of Newcastle. It was a bitter battle—lots of hops in those Scottish ales—but the best men won. Namely, all of us.

By contrast, Americans for the most part don't have a sense of pride in the native product, much less an interest in beer chauvinism. This is not to say the denizens of the British Isles and Ireland aren't every bit as parochial as Americans, but at least they have better beer. Americans, however, *are* a people ever in flux—and gradually, over the past decade or so, they have begun to covet better beer. This has been partly a result of the shrinkage of the American beer industry—not in volume certainly, but in numbers of brewing companies—and the *sameness* of so many domestic brands. And while "light" beers have revolutionized the industry, they have also been viewed by some beer-lovers as yet another milestone in the progress of American beer to less and less taste.

There are also other factors: widespread travel abroad by Americans, which has prompted interest in the

# A
# Romance
# with
# Beer

availability of foreign beers; the switch from spirits to wine and beer because of health reasons; the growing interest in drinking beer with food, especially with the spicy cuisines of Mexico and Asia; the rapidly escalating appreciation of both food and drink; the "publization" of many American bars; and the delicious snobbery intrinsic to drinking something the neighbors don't know about. Yet what is also being imported into America, along with hundreds of foreign brands, is not just other peoples' love affair with beer but with the mystique of beer itself—its legends and lore, its fascinating history, its worldwide popularity. On a practical level, Americans are voting for more taste, more variety of taste, more diversity of choice.

The evidence of this slowly building movement is manifold. Supermarkets all

# A
# Romance
# with
# Beer

around America, which once stocked a dozen or so imported beers, now may offer three or four times that number. Gourmet shops and specialty food shops raise the ante by another few dozen. And all around the country there are bars specializing in huge beer lists. Current king of the heap: Washington, D.C.'s Brickskeller Saloon, with about 500 brands!

As the interest in foreign beers has grown in America, so have the numbers of imports—they now number in the hundreds —and the fabled "melting pot" has become unique in that respect. Only in Germany are there to be found more brands of beer, but no German city offers scores of different beers. Yet Americans are far from understanding that central to the mystique of beer are the various brewing styles and the wide diversity of tastes they provide. Beer, it can be argued, is no less complex a subject than wine. And it would help educate the public's palate if there were equivalents to wine bars devoted to notable beers—not merely large numbers of beers—where styles of beer could be compared and interesting or exotic beers tasted, along with food selections that are especially complemented by beer. But until this happy event takes place, it is the job of the importers to try and expand beer knowledge in America.

At present, I believe, there is only one importer making a concerted effort to educate not only the public, but also the people who sell their product to the public, in the wide, wide world of beer. Merchant du Vin, a Seattle-based company established in 1978 by Elizabeth Purser and Charles Finkel, both veterans of the wine trade, is marketing "a selection of imported beers, primarily from family-owned breweries, which reflect the local traditions of the countries and regions of their origin." The beers are said to be all-natural and exactly

# A Romance with Beer

the same as in their place of origin. Finkel likes to use the term "hand-crafted"; his are not assembly-line beers. And certainly the firm's selections are exotic as well as eclectic—Diekirch Pilsener from Luxembourg, Aass Bok from Norway, Kaiserdom Rauchbier, a smoked beer from *Deutchland*, Lindemans Gueuze Lambic from Belgium, Samuel Smith Taddy Porter from England—and the marketing concept of distinguishing between the two basic brewing types (lagers and ales) is both useful and informative. It's simply more interesting to taste beers of a similar style from various nations than to taste beers strictly by nationality.

## Beer Tastings

Away from the beer trade, a few wine-lovers have been tasting beer with the same fidelity of purpose previously reserved for the fruit of the grape. By far the leader in this movement has been Les Amis du Vin (The Friends of Wine), the largest wine society in America, with a burgeoning number of chapters abroad. Ron Fonte, founder of Les Amis du Vin and publisher-editor of *The Friends of Wine,* the society's bimonthly magazine, has a simple enough explanation for this unprecedented development: "Most of our chapters have been in existence about ten years, and once you taste all the wines once, twice, three times, you want to explore other taste experiences. Suddenly, with more imported beers on the market, wine-lovers have realized that they have the same fascination for beers—that they have as much range and complexity, as well as different styles, and that the whole fun part is to compare all these different beers as you would wines."

All over America, chapters of Les Amis du Vin, as well as other wine apprecia-

# A Romance with Beer

# A Romance with Beer

tion societies, have been holding beer tastings in relaxed settings—out-of-doors and in pubby places or other casual eateries—and at seminars and formal dinners. Most tastings are blind—beers are decanted and identified only by numbers. And in some instances the complex University of California at Davis' twenty-point scoring system for wine is applied. Other tastings place more emphasis (eight points) on flavor, and a maximum of three points each to aroma, carbonation, clarity, appearance of head, body and flavor. In another sophisticated scoring system, a maximum of five points each is given for body, foam, color, aroma, taste, bitterness and flavor.

However, don't let all this deter you. Beer tastings are neither solemn nor forbidding events. They're fun as well as educational. For instance, I've held beer tastings in connection with this book, but none so sublime as the one I recently attended at the gracious home of Mr. James D. Robertson in Fair Haven, New Jersey. By profession an electronics engineer, Jim has the look of the scholar about him, and that he is—of both wine and beer. He heads the Monmouth Wine Society, an organization with 600 members in twenty states, and has written *The Great American Beer Book,* an exemplary tome replete with tasting notes. As this book is being written, Robertson is completing an even more ambitious work—tasting notes on all domestic American brands as well as the available imports—for which I am providing the Introduction. You see, rather than regarding each other as rivals, we are both lovers not only of beer but of serious beer-talk. And we both want to see much more beer scholarship, not just an occasional book title. And beer tastings in every hamlet and village!

In the interim, however, welcome to the romance and protocol of serious beer

# A
# Romance
# with
# Beer

tasting. An average tasting may involve as many as fifteen beers, with each taster receiving no more than two ounces of each brand. No one spits out the beer, but it isn't necessary to consume all of it. Even so, this would amount to only two-and-a-half bottles of beer per tasting—not an awesome figure. Even if there are fewer brands, however, the two ounces are enough to taste the beer—more would cause difficulty in distinguishing between beers. As for the identity of the beers, ideally the host arranges it so that someone else pours them into glasses and he—the host—doesn't know which beers are actually being served at any one time. That's part of the fun.

As for food to clean the palate, the obvious choices are not appropriate. Potato chips, pretzels, and any other salty items are out because they affect your palate too much. The same, alas, is the complaint with certain foods that are thought to go well with beer. For example, liverwurst goes dandy with some beers—but not with others—so it's not for tastings. Certain breads might be all right, but they tend to fill you up, as does the beer. Plain popcorn does the trick best.

Temperature is a bit of a problem. Your refrigerator is not operating at 45 degrees Fahrenheit so you'll have to experiment with the amount of time needed for full lager appreciation. Try taking the beer out of the refrigerator ten minutes ahead of tasting time for lagers—they can't get too warm that way, and if more time is needed the pouring and serving should take care of that. More time for ales, darker beers—don't become hysterical over these getting too warm. You'll find their flavor occasionally enhanced by higher temperatures.

For a tasting, ordinary wine glasses are okay—the beers look attractive—but flute and tulip glasses do the job better because

# A Romance with Beer

they capture the "nose" of the beer and help keep the head as well. Jim Robertson has found some French pilsner stemware that answers both esthetic and utilitarian needs. These glasses can be held by the stem if the taster wants to keep the beer cool or by the bowl if the beer can stand warming up to fulfill its potential. Equally important, the order of serving should be from light to more flavorful beers, which means pairing lagers or pilsners (Jim regards these terms as interchangeable), then ales, then darker beers. A basic tasting, therefore, might begin with low-calorie beers, then go on to popularly priced lagers, then premium lagers and imports, then ales and darker lagers—higher density beers with their roasted malt flavor that are a step up in intensity on the palate. The last beers one tastes are stouts and porters. A taster can drink very "hoppy," very pungent beers and then fully appreciate beers that have been made from roasted or toasted malts, but not the other way around. "The malty beers have more of a saturating effect on your palate than do the hoppy varieties," Jim observes, glass in hand, reminding me at once of both Craig Claiborne and Brendan Behan.

# A Romance with Beer

Tonight's event, however, is hardly typical. It's a feat of logistics. Included are two new imports from South America and a rare (in the Northeast) one, Corona, from Mexico. The only American entry is San Francisco's Anchor Steam Brewery's Our Special Ale 1980, a limited bottling. From Canada, there are Labatt's Super Bock and John Labatt's Extra Stock Ale, plus a Carlsberg Gold made there by Carling O'Keefe. From Germany, there is a Bavarian beer, Maisel Fest (a special festival beer); and from Kulmbach, three beers, including the fabled Erste Kulminator Urtyp 28 Malt Liquor. It has to be called a malt liquor in America because it's 13.2 percent alcohol by volume and is listed in *The Guinness Book of Records* as the world's strongest beer. There's also an Easter beer from Denmark and another called Green Rooster, the label of which proclaims: "Lean, Green and Mean." Jim is amused by the label, but finds the beer's pale lime green color "atrocious."

Color is important, you see, because everyone is expected to offer their opinions on the appearance, "nose" (bouquet and aroma), taste, and aftertaste of the beers. The appearance has to be attractive, with color and density appropriate to the style of beer, and reasonably clear. Sometimes, in certain imports, cloudiness is a good sign, indicating cranky yeast cells still trying to do their fermentation job. Whereas at other times cloudiness may be caused by matter that will be detrimental to flavor.

Next, the "nose," which is composed of two elements. "The aroma is the nasal sensation caused by the product's ingredients and the bouquet results from the by-products of fermentation," Jim explains to a guest, adding that the negative elements to be aware of include excessive yeastiness, sourness, staleness and skunkiness. Does

# 𝕬 𝕽omance 𝔴ith 𝕭eer

he actually mean "skunkiness"? Yes, the same smell many of us have experienced while driving on a highway where some unfortunate creature has met its end.

Put in simple terms, the beer should smell clean, pure, beery, with appropriate (to the type) presence of hops and malts. Put less simply, but of no small fascination: "The two major components to the 'nose' are the malt and the hops. There are bittering hops, which add body and some bite and shelf life, and aromatic hops, which produce complex smells. Clover in particular is one smell you may get, but there are also

*Hops*

# A Romance with Beer

sagey hops and ones that are almost floral and other kinds that are spicy or citrus in nature. Actually, it takes a fairly complicated blend of both kinds of hops to get the full measure of the aroma plus the substance for the taste. Somehow aromatic hops don't do much for your palate.''

Palates, of course, are highly personal, but Jim believes it helps to taste in two stages. The first taste will tell you if the beer has sufficient body, what degree of sweetness it has, how much carbonation (small bubbles, please, as in fine champagne), how strong it is, how much hoppiness exists and whether there's sufficient maltiness. Quaffing, the second stage of serious tasting, gives one the taste while swallowing, plus the aftertaste. It isn't vital to quaff all the beer, but at least some must be swallowed to critique the aftertaste.

"If the beer has no aftertaste or a very brief one, it finishes poorly," Jim tells that same guest. "If the aftertaste is sour, metallic, or bitter, it finishes badly. As you swallow, the palate sensation should be mostly of malt, with some faint sweetness, and even fainter bitterness from the hops. An ideal brew has balance throughout, with a taste remaining in the mouth that is pleasant in all respects. It may be the only recollection of the entire experience."

Perhaps, but now it's scoring time. From his on-going comments, Jim has found most of the beers worthy of admiration, but he finds no reason to disagree with the group's ranking of Maisel Fest as the top performer. Still, I get the feeling that he had a special affection for that "Lean, Green and Mean" number from Denmark. "It's a beautifully done, highly hopped beer with lots of character," he opines. "Very tasty." On the other hand, the Anchor was "delicious."

# A Romance with Beer

He's right, of course, but it really wasn't necessary—only fun—to pick a winner from this crowd, because there really weren't any clinkers. Ah, brave new world, that's finally bringing the Old World mystique of beer to America!

And no need to worry about vintages. Great beers are for today....

*Beer tasters at Anheuser-Busch*

Beer!
A
Short
History

# Beer! A Short History

There are anthropologists who hold that man actually began the formal cultivation of grain not for the baking of breads, but for the brewing, however primitive, of beer. It's known that certain pre-agricultural societies produced fermented beverages and that all known agricultural societies, whether of antiquity or not, have in common the production of alcoholic beverages. The first accidental alcholic beverage (made by nature rather than man) may have been mead fermented from honey; wine, fermented from the juice of grapes; or beer, created when some free-floating yeast cells came into contact with grain being soaked to prepare some form of prehistoric bread.

Such considerations aside, we know that beer became the most widely used of the earliest alcoholic beverages simply because grains were more widely available than the grapes or the other fruits used for fermented beverages. Beer was quaffed by ancient peoples from around the globe, including the Chinese and Incas, the African Negro and white Berber races, the Babylonians, Assyrians, Egyptians and Hebrews, plus the Teutons, Saxons and tribes of Trans-Caucasia. There is a well-preserved series of tablets from the ancient city of Babylon documenting—possibly for the first time—how the peoples of Mesopotamia, the country lying between the Euphrates and Tigris rivers, knew how to prepare malt and barley and apparently knew how to develop yeast strains for fermentation purposes twenty centuries before the birth of Christ. The *Shu-King* and *Shi-King*, 300-year-old Chinese documents, mention a brew known as *kiu,* but not how it was produced. It may simply have been fermented millet and then later on, a combination of millet and rice and wheat plus aromatic plants and flavoring. What isn't

# Beer! A Short History

known is whether it was a pre- or after-dinner drink, or whether it went well with Chinese food.

In both the older Mesopotamian cultures, as well as in Egypt of the time, women were the master brewers and priestesses as well, because beer had definite religious associations. In 2,100 B.C., that original male chauvinist monarch, King Hammurabi, gave the brewing jobs to men and let women continue running the taverns. They also kept their priestess jobs. In Egypt, however, the vital female connection with beer continued a good deal longer. Although beer had been invented by Ra, the Sun God, the goddess Iris was the patroness of brewing, which was a pretty important assignment if Ra's invention was to go anywhere. At the mortal level, everyone, including kids, drank beer; it was regarded as an item of economic exchange as well as a token for binding official agreements. And unofficial agreements as well: When a young man offered a young lady a serious sip of beer, they were considered betrothed.

*Ancient Egyptians making beer*

# Beer! A Short History

The role of beer in Egyptian life as well as in the social lives of the gods is so well established that when Alexander the Great came over from Greece and was kind enough to install a dynasty of Macedonian rulers, the production of beer, its sale and consumption were placed under royal rule. This seems, in retrospect, a wrongheaded move. Both the Greeks and Romans, heavy wine drinkers, were eventually defeated in titanic warfare by beer-swilling warriors. Greece may have had an excuse, because it hung around the area of the Mediterranean too much before setting out to conquer parts east. But the Romans ran into local beer cultures in Spain, among the people of what is now Spain, the Gauls and the Celtics. Some advanced combat training while fortified by beer and perhaps the Roman legions would have handled the Teutonic armies of Attila the Hun with more success. Perhaps not, too, because official Teuton beer sessions of a sedentary nature made the formidable demand that the participants not leave the table until everyone was done—or else done in.

Attila the Hun and his swarmy hordes do not seem to have been the sort much given to formal toasting—in point of fact the word *toast* is a seventeenth century creation based on the practice of dipping a piece of warm bread into wine to improve its flavor. But to the ancient Saxons and their equally ferocious neighbors to the north, the Norsemen, most drinking occasions required toasting. And among the Norsemen, since most every occasion required drinking, toasts were made to the just married, the recently departed, the forthcoming harvest and the newly arrived Norseperson. Furthermore, any meeting, secular or religious, was regarded as an "ale" (actually *oel*) because that was the impetus for accomplishing something at these sessions and the binding

# Beer!
# A
# Short
# History

fluid for their legitimacy. Any contract drawn up at an "ale," regardless of nature, was considered legally solid to the point whereby "beer house testimony" became a part of the Norse legal language.

By contrast, the early Britons mostly drank mead and hard cider, which apparently helped them fight off neither colds nor the marauding Norsemen. But once the Romans gave them the benefit of their invading ways, clearly an improvement on the mariners from the west who only came by to knock heads and take things home, the Britons began to live in hamlets and then towns and villages. *Tabernae*—taverns to the Romans, but alehouses to the locals—began to appear as pit stops between the small outposts of civilization, dispensing wine as well as ale. With the Anglo-Saxon takeover in the fifth century and thereafter, ale became the national drink of England. During medieval times, consumption was stated to be as high as eight quarts a day per adult, and the Scots and Irish, busily developing their whiskies, surely must have blanched at the unseemly display of intake.

But it wasn't all fun 'n pains. As in Scandinavia, the business transacted at any "ale" was entirely legal. When England became Christianized for good, the religious blandishments included much concern for over-excessive drinking. At the same time a series of inns—one of the progenitors of the modern pub—was established to ensure that no deserving pilgrim would go thirsty. And to assure patronage, the monks and nuns made the very best brews to be found in England.

However, to ensure their own source of levity, the laity of England established alehouses in each village—the other model for the pub—in addition to continuing the lusty practice of home brewing. But there were no thriving commercial breweries be-

# Beer! A Short History

cause neither the Crown nor the church wanted to give up the tax and consumer income, respectively, from this alementary source of revenue. Indeed, the church managed to make some areas free of any source of ale save its own premises.

Interestingly enough, much the same thing was happening on the Continent. Monasteries were also citadels of brewing. In Germany the fame of some religious orders grew to prestigious heights. Munich's Augustiner and Paulaner are two examples of this kind of religious dedication. As a wise and intuitive ruler, Charlemagne—acting as king of the Franks and ruler of the Holy Roman Empire—established a code of rules governing royal brewing centers and a policy of letting the church have monopoly markets.

Cologne became a major brewing center, as did Hamburg, Bremen and Lubeck in the north, coastal cities outside Charlemagne's jurisdiction. These were followed by local brewing fiefdoms in Hanover, Dortmund, Frankfurt, Muenster, Nuremberg and of course, Munich. After the Thirty Years War, a series (1618-48) of religious wars that deeply divided the German "nation," brewing harmony became centered, at least in terms of fame, in the Bavarian city, where brewers, emulating masons, carpenters and other master craftsmen, formed guilds with high standards for practice of their trade. For almost a century, first the city government and then the Bavarian state issued ever more comprehensive regulations concerning beer. This culminated in 1516's *Rheinheitsgebot,* the famous Bavarian code of purity forbidding any ingredients other than barley, yeast, hops and water being used in the brewing of beer. The law remains in application today to all German beers sold in Germany, and is adhered to as well by Norway, Switzerland and

# Beer! A Short History

Luxembourg. It is a good idea whose time has never left us.

At the same time great beer traditions were evolving in England and Germany, there were foaming counterparts in other European regions. The beers of Bohemia, a Slavic nation that was once part of Austria but now is Czechoslovakian territory, fully rivaled those of Germany in fame. Usually wheat or barley beers, but often given exotic flavors via the use of herbs and spices, they owed their distinctive character to the renowned Czech hops, cultivated since 859 A.D. The area's rulers, particularly the Holy Roman Emperor Wenceslas of Bohemia, recognized the special worth of the beers being brewed in Pilsen, Prague and Zatec, among other towns, and made it not only illegal, but a crime punishable by death, to leave the country with hop cuttings. In the 1600s, the Bohemian tavern began to rival the local brews in celebrity because of the "Eat, drink and be merry and repeat same" philosophy practiced on the premises.

# Beer!
# A
# Short
# History

However, the Thirty Years War shut down the merry growth of the Bohemian brewing trade for a considerable period of time—one city saved itself from the attacking Swedish army by bartering its continued safety in exchange for a small army of beer barrels—and Bohemian brewers would never be the same idiosyncratic band. The 1800s saw a change from wheat beers to barley beers and the adopting of German bottom-fermentation lager techniques. This proved nowhere so felicitous a transformation as in Pilsen, where a band of 250 families, unhappy with the local product, formed a cooperative known as the Citizens Brewery. Their new product, Pilsner Urquell, did more to establish Czech beer's fame than any earlier brew.

At the same time, a mighty brewing tradition was long flowering in the small nations of Belgium and Holland, where monks working in Europe in the tenth and eleventh centuries had spread the gospel about beer as well as God, although certainly not in that order. Soon enough the consumption of beer was enjoying the same kind of familial and socializing associations it did in Scandinavia, England, Germany and Bohemia. In Holland, *Kinderbier* was served to celebrate christenings and *Leedbier* to express sorrow at funerals. And families were nicknamed after their associations with the beer trade, such names as Brouwers and Bruwers and later Bestbier and Bierman, can be traced to the froth-hearted practice.

On state occasions, however, the national affection for beer was marked by the creation of elaborate beer mugs for use at these ceremonial events, and some of these can be seen today in the surviving guild halls and medieval buildings of Holland. These often towering tributes of beerdom may also be seen in Brussels' elegant *Grand Place*, the

# Beer!
# A
# Short
# History

glistening center of town, where the *Maison des Brasseurs* is the only remaining guild hall still operative as it was in past centuries. The building, which helps form what is surely one of Europe's most charming but also impressive public squares, also houses a beer museum presumably haunted by Cambrinus or Gambrinus, or several other people, all of whom were either the King of Beer in Europe or the patron saint of beer for all Christendom. The Dutch also make some claims as to the nationality of this personage, and his name is inscribed in saintly context on an ancient monastery stone in Bavaria. But the Belgians seem to have the best case. I am indebted to Frederick Birmingham, the well-known editor and author, for this insight in the mystery: "The truth of the Gambrinus legend seems to point more precisely to a man who actually lived. One portrait of Gambrinus labels him as 'King of Flanders and Brabant.' We do know that a famous Baron of Brabant was a certain Jan Primus, who was not only a noted warrior and a local hero, but also renowned for his capacity. He is said to have quaffed seventy-two quarts of beer at one sitting. In addition, he was president of the Brussels Guild of Brewers from 1261 to 1294, with his portrait hanging in the great hall. If you say Jan Primus fast enough and figure out that a man of that name was the champion drinker of his time, you have the right kind of start to launch a patron saint of beer called Gambrinus."

In this spirit, therefore, the Belgians developed an astonishing beer culture for a nation so small, and it is not national chauvinism but self-flattery that causes them to describe their better brews as the   Burgundy of Belgium." Not only is their range of beers broad and truly innovative, but their passion for noble brews is evidenced every day in the thousands of cafes that line the

# Beer! A Short History

boulevards and streets of the nation's cities. According to England's Michael Jackson, there are 60,000 of them, or as many pubs existing in England, a nation of five times Belgium's population. One beer emporium per every 167 persons—that's a serious kingdom of beer, with or without the good King Gambrinus.

Meanwhile, back in Merrie Old England, another king, Henry the Second, had levied the first national beer tax in 1188 to help underwrite the Crusades, but his son, Henry the Third, showed a lot of political savvy by ordering price controls on both bread and ale, staples of daily life. His edict, the Assize of Bread and Ale, remained in effect for three centuries and inspired the creation of the ale-taster, who was summoned each time an alehouse had new brew to sell. He'd pour a tankard of the ale on a wooden bench and plop down upon it, wearing his

# Beer!
# A
# Short
# History

special leather breeches. If, after a pre-
scribed period of time, he tried to get up and
his breeches tried to prevent him, it meant
that the brew had too much sugar in it and
was therefore on the weak side—despite its
obvious adhesive qualities. If the sugar had
been properly converted into alcohol, then
the ale was strong enough and deserving of
official approval. Not the most scientific
system, perhaps, but England was now becoming a nation of cities and the alehouses
or pubs—public places where food and
drink was served—represented something of
a population explosion themselves. Until a
system for licensing each pub was developed, the ale-taster was the only means of
preventing the proprietor of a drinking establishment from putting something over on
the public—in other words, flying by the
seat of his pants.

In the fifteenth century, the first
commercial brewing company was formed
by royal charter. Much brewing was still
done at home, as well as in the establish-
ments today known as "locals." But the
great brewing families—the Barclays,
Courages, Trumans, Watneys and Whit-
breads in England and the Youngers in Scotland—hadn't yet started their dynasties. Yet
all around the country much more brewing
was brewing, small concerns appearing and
producing their local beers, with one of
them—Burton Ale from Burton-on-Trent
near Stafford—gaining a wide and enviable
reputation. The discovery that the waters of
the Trent River, running over rocks of gyp-
sum, helped produce an ale of unusual
brightness and clarity eventually led to the
knowledge that water used for brewing beer
should be hard rather than soft, and light in
organic matter. But that was a scientific rev-
elation, and back then Burton Ale was con-
tent with a sensibility that transcended any
ready explanation.

# Beer! A Short History

The Britons remained devoted to their unhopped ale, even though it rapidly went sour—whatever didn't get consumed when the ale was fresh—while hops were already being utilized in many European nations both to flavor and help preserve beer. Hops and beer from Holland were being imported by the Dutch community in London and eventually, although the battle was to rage on for much of the fifteenth century, beer won out over ale. Oh, the Britons still brewed a distinctive drink  and called it by the old name, but the sweet ales of the Middle Ages are only brewed today at a few colleges at Oxford and Cambridge, as a kind of semi-scholarly recreation of the past.

When England began colonizing America, it was partly the Elizabethan Age, a time when England's love affair with its ale was at regal heights—when she was traveling about the land, Her Majesty had a chap of great good taste travel on ahead and make sure a noble brew would be waiting for her—and it is little wonder that this affection for ale came over with the colonialist. It's known that the Pilgrims landed at Plymouth Rock because their provisions, including ale, were dangerously low, but it isn't known whether the ale was aboard because the Pilgrims wouldn't leave England without it or whether it was there because it kept better than water. In either case, home brewing followed the English from England. But the first brewery in the New Country was set up in 1612 by two Dutchmen in a log structure on the southern tip of Manhattan Island. More fort than settlement, New Amsterdam soon enough included a Brouwer Street and a lively beer trade. Amongst the English, commercial brewing was at first confined to taverns and alehouses, but Connecticut and Rhode Island had a number of breweries operating by 1640. Corn, wheat and rye, as well as barley,

# Beer! A Short History

were utilized—but those grains needed for food supplies as export items were forbidden for brewing as circumstance required. Still, a brewing industry was encouraged both for economic reasons and because beer was regarded as the alcoholic drink of moderation. But hard cider fell by the wayside, in terms of becoming a real industry; rum was replaced by native whiskies, mostly from Pennsylvania; and ale (henceforth beer) was the preferred potable of the gentry, along with wine or sherry when available.

William Penn, who gave the state his name, was possibly as well known for the size of the brewing vats on his estate in Pennsbury as he was for his potential role in American history. George Washington brewed his own beer at Mount Vernon and his recipe for "small beer" is on display at the New York Public Library. Thomas Jefferson not only brewed with gusto, he collected every book on the subject, and these, along with the rest of his extensive library, were the basic collection of books used in forming the Library of Congress.

*Beer was delivered to the inns in small open carts.*

# Beer!
# A
# Short
# History

Even more significantly, however, brewers and tavern-keepers were highly respected citizens and they were to assume important military positions in the American Revolution and civil roles in the nation's young government. Indeed, the taverns themselves were the citadels of the desire for freedom, local headquarters for the revolutionary Sons of Liberty.

Following the war, as the country gradually began to expand, brewing slowly left the eastern seaboard and moved toward the Mississippi and beyond. But no new brewery, whether established in Chicago or St. Louis or Milwaukee, seemed to rival the reputation for fine beer engendered by some Philadelphia brews, in particular the porter made by Robert Hare. There is no small irony, therefore, in the fact that a subsequent Philadelphia brewer named John Wagner began producing lager in 1840 from yeast he'd brought over from the Bavarian brewery at which he'd been *braumeister,* and lager began to enjoy its first popularity in America. Wagner's enormous success just happened to neatly coincide with the arrival of a very large number of German emigrants who had left their homeland for economic and political reasons. When they settled in communities from Brooklyn to St. Louis to Texas, they provided a ready market for the German-style brew they thought they had left behind them.

By 1880 the Schaffer brothers, Frederick and Maximilian, were enjoying a triumph in New York, as were Joseph Schlitz and Frederick Pabst and Miller in Milwaukee and Eberhard Anheuser and Adolphus Busch in St. Louis. There were 431 breweries by 1850; there would be an all-time high of 4,131 in 1873, and lager was the fueling propellant. Lager swept aside the British style of beer like so much used suds. And at the same time, it must be speculated, lager

# Beer! A Short History

helped inspire the image of beer as a proletarian drink, the beverage of immigrants and common laborers. Nor did the next wave of immigration, from Ireland, do anything to dispel the symbol of beer as the common man's drink. When it comes to drink, America has long been status-conscious; beer is just now beginning to regain the high status it originally enjoyed here. Strange are the ways of democracy!

Even stranger, indeed, when you consider that America played host to that odious experiment known as Prohibition. At first beer, as the temperance drink, was to have been excluded from the act. But anti-saloon sentiment, along with the sense that beer, as a German drink, was associated with the Kaiser and his armies, caused it to be included.

*Raid on a moonshine operation during Prohibition*

Prohibition took a dreadful toll on the national morality and on the brewing industry in particular. There was something called "near beer," so bad that it caused humorous ripostes to the effect that whoever called it that was a rotten judge of distance.

43

# Beer! A Short History

When the Great Dry Spell was ended by an act of Congress in 1933, President Franklin D. Roosevelt pleaded that saloons never be allowed to appear on the American landscape again—and brewers rushed out their beer to sell in institutions that were no longer saloons. Americans quaffed a million barrels of beer during the first twenty-four-hour period of freedom from want. Yet the American brewing industry, despite this surge of instant enthusiasm, did not recover its pre-Prohibition volume until 1940, and the number of brewers has continued to diminish over the years. In 1950, Wisconsin had fifty breweries, yet today there aren't that many in the entire country. An interesting development, however, is the establishment of so-called "boutique" breweries around the country, producing their own styles of beer. This is similar to the wine industry, and is at least a refreshing antidote, however modest, to the giantism of the American brewing industry.

But beer is back, let there be no disputation about that. Consumption in the United States is double that of 1953. Significantly more Americans are drinking beer than ever before. The concerns of waist-watchers have no doubt put some numbers on the side of beer, but beer is also becoming "in," chic, trendy, whatever it takes to get it into the very best refrigerators. And to exercise a bit of reverse snobbism, we serious beer mavens don't mind this democratization of beer at all—just so long as it continues to provide more diversity of choice and expansion of good taste. After all, the joy of beer hasn't been such a secret for the past 10,000 years and it's about time these folks caught up with the rest of the world.

# Beer!
# A
# Short
# History

*Crowd waiting for the end of Prohibition,*
*Times Square 1933*

# Beer
# Basics

1869

S. LIEBMANN'S SON'S MALT HOUSE

Williamsburg, L.I.

# Beer Basics

**B**arley malt. Yeast. Hops. And water. These, to the beer purist, are the Holy Brew of great beer. They have been the classic ingredients of beer for centuries, and I am not aware that the addition of anything else improves upon this time-honored beer formulation. A few German brewers produce a weiss- or weizenbier, wheat beers that are served as a complement to desert or, to some palates, could *be* a dessert. For example, the former are taken with essence of woodruff, a sweet, aromatic herb, and raspberry juice or syrup, the latter with lemon. Not a taste treat for everyone surely, but certainly a taste event. Wheat beers do not lack for some popularity in Belgium as well—as a nation the Belgians are probably the most eccentric of beer drinkers in addition to competing with the West Germans and Czechs as highest per capita consumers in the beer universe.

Wheat beers, however, are traditional beers. No one added other grains to them to produce a lighter beer. By contrast, American beers have become lighter and lighter, with the addition of grain adjuncts such as corn and rice being utilized to brew the sort of pale-colored, light-bodied beer that currently dominates the market. However, as the beer purist will churlishly point out—given the slightest provocation or opportunity to do so—light also means less. Less flavor and less of what has made beer traditionally taste like—well, beer.

I am a member of this community of churls. American brewers may argue that they now produce a different beer, not a less flavorful one, but to me the difference *is* less flavor. If it were otherwise, the brewers themselves would not be bringing out their super premiums, there would be no boutique brewers—tiny companies with a large interest in good beer—springing up around the country, and imports wouldn't be grow-

# Beer
# Basics

ing at such a significant rate. However, I concede that the relative merits of light vs. heavy bodied beer are rather more subjective. As are differences in flavor; not every beer-lover enjoys the same tastes in beer, and it would be a boring beverage if they did.

From an esthetic or sensory perception—how beer looks, smells and tastes—*why* use any crops other than barley unless they improve flavor or else provide an interesting alternative to traditional tastes? There is a kind of philosophical issue here: Did American brewers create the taste for a

*Kegs being filled and sealed on the draught line*

# Beer Basics

lighter beer (I exclude here the Miller "lite" type beers, obviously a remarkable marketing phenomenon), or did they respond to it? In any case, other, less expensive crops are being used as adjuncts to barley; chemical agents are used to affect the head and other aspects of the beer. Also a goodly number of additives play their role in shelf life, which is a real problem for a relatively fragile food product. They prevent the beer from gushing out of the bottle, as well as all sorts of other beer vices.

These additives indeed represent a kind of scientific progress in the centuries-old art and new science of brewing. But, truthfully, can anyone serious about "suds" cheer on behalf of corn syrup and grapefruit oil being added, along with as many as thirty other "wonder drugs," to enhance flavor? Barley became preferred for beer in the first place because it wasn't very good for making bread but absolutely the best crop for making beer. Brewers over the ages came to realize just how barley not only provides the basic taste of beer, but its color, its head and its body—in the person of malto-dextrins and protein, although those folksy terms weren't used by the people who began to get serious about consistent brewing standards a half-millenium or so ago. It's just as well, in

# Beer Basics

point of fact, that they weren't conversant with carbon dioxide, which is today used in some cheap brews to provide the carbonation that should be produced by the beer itself. Such modern techniques, in the name of progress, offend on two counts: They make the beer gassy and inspire the bladder to become no less edgy than the average militant beer purist.

These complaints having been registered, let me point out that brewing is not an easy process. It is no small matter to brew a consistently high quality product. Brewers' yeasts are living organisms, fungi that can behave unpredictably and go beyond their job of causing fermentation to influence taste. Pasteurization, generally done with beers that are going to be exported or sold over a wide marketing area, helps preserve the beer, among other things, but it also destroys some (however small) degree of flavor. It has to—beer is no longer a soup, after all, at this stage in the brewing process. Most of the foreign brands being sent to America, therefore, are pasteurized, the exceptions being some highly hopped beers that are aided by a lot of personal supervision at the brewery and enjoy far more than the usual shelf life. Hops, in addition to imparting a necessary contrasting bitterness to what would otherwise be a sweet drink, also have an important preservative function.

Hops also add aroma to beer. Before the hops come into play, however, the much-bruited barley must be prepared for their arrival. This involves two critical steps. First, the barley must be steeped in water and permitted to germinate (sprout). This process is then arrested by a heat-drying procedure. If dark beer is to be produced, the barley malt—the dried, sprouted grains—will be first roasted before being mixed with hot water to produce a mash

hot water tank

brew kettle

hops

hops extractor

mash filter

holding tank

filter

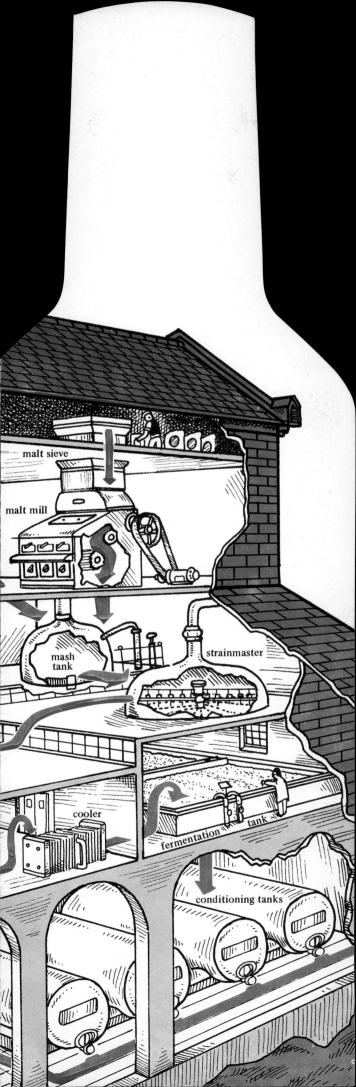

malt sieve

malt mill

mash tank

strainmaster

cooler

fermentation tank

conditioning tanks

(called a "wort") in which cereal starches are converted into fermentable sugars and proteins.

Thus far water has been mentioned twice and any serious beer scholar is familiar with the ecstatic claims made on behalf of the water used in certain beers. It used to be true that breweries were often established near sources of water because certain waters had mineral qualities that helped produce more attractive beer. But today all water used for beer undergoes distillation to ensure purity. Often the water has to be chemically adjusted to facilitate the fermentation process, so if those remarkable mineral qualities survive in any modern beers, they are remarkable indeed.

We left the mash in the mash kettle. After filtration, the malt extract is introduced to hops and the two of them are sent into the brew kettle, the fermentation tank. The best hops in the world are said to be those from Czechoslovakia, but most European brewers use a variety of hops. American companies use a blend of the unnecessarily bitter domestic hops plus imported varieties. However, hops experiments in Washington state promise to produce a native species rivaling Europe's best.

To make the rest of the brewing process simple without being simplistic, the addition of specially cultivated yeast in the fermentation tank breaks down the sugar molecules into alcohol and little bubbles of carbon dioxide. Then the "green beer" is aged in storage tanks. If the beer is given enough time in aging—an event, alas, becoming increasingly rare—not only will the flavor improve for weeks or months, but a secondary fermentation will help produce a naturally effervescent beer with small, non-gassy bubbles. There is also *krausening,* the addition of bubbly younger beer to that beer ready for packaging, and the injection

# Beer Basics

of carbonation taken from the fermentation tanks into the aged brew. These are both honorable, although not superior, methods of ensuring carbonation, but the zapping of beer with $CO_2$, as is done with soft drinks, produces a beverage not worthy of affection, much less respect.

Much of the rest of the brewing process is cosmetic. Another filtration provides clarity to the beer by removing yeast and protein matter. Fining agents are sometimes used to "polish" the beer to even more brilliant clarity. The beer is then pasteurized before being packaged in bottles or cans. If it's intended to be drawn from kegs for use on draft, it usually isn't pasteurized in America and is given a "flash pasteurization" (20 seconds of steam) abroad.

To understand the distinction between ale and beer, we have to go back to the fermentation tank. Beer—lagers, pilsners, many dark brews—results from bottom fermentation. The yeast is allowed to settle at the bottom of the tank and do its vital bubbly work at the level. Ale, by contrast, is top fermented at higher temperatures than beer and the end result is a different kettle of brew. This is the elemental distinction between the two principal types of beer made in the world, but let's examine them a bit more closely.

Lagers and pilsner beers are very closely related and very often the same, the chief difference being that made by the label. Lager derives from the German verb *lagern* (to store). German monks used to store their *bier* in mountain caves during summer months. As for *pilsners*, (also *pilseners, pils*), they are named after the excellent beer brewed in Pilsen, Czechoslovakia, for the past 700 years. The term became generic, but the finest example remains Pilsner Urquell from Pilsen. Both types are pale in color, relatively light in

# Beer Basics

body, crisp and with dry, effervescent tastes. European pilsners are, among other things, more distinctly hoppy than American lagers.

Dark beers—at least those on the Continent—are also lagers. They are usually heavier in taste, sweeter, more malty and aromatic than light lagers. Germany's *bock* beers are fabled examples of this category at its lustiest level of color, strength and body weight.

Ale—often referred to as "bitter" in England—can range in color from amber to ruby to off-brown and sometimes even darker. As a rule, they are heavier-bodied than all but the most Germanic dark lagers and a few other special brews, and have a firmer hop flavor and aroma in balance with their maltiness.

Porters, not easily found, were originally a local London product that, legend has it, was much favored by porters. A kind of hybrid beer—dark brown, it is as heavy as most ales but less hoppy and has the intense maltiness one finds in stouts. Today porter is made in the ale tradition by England's Samuel Smith Brewery and as a lager most other places.

Stouts are in the ale family, and the darkest, richest, maltiest of all regularly produced beers. This is usually modified by a pronounced hoppy taste, but not always, a few stouts being definitely on the sweet side.

"Malt liquor" is a term conjured up to describe beers that exceed the legal alcoholic levels—5 percent in the United States—of that nation. They are most often made as lagers, but the American version can be either sweetish or more bitter than traditional lagers.

Within this general framework, there are fascinating variations. We will become acquainted with them in the globe-trotting section on beers. Don't hold your breath,

# Beer Basics

but instead pour yourself a splendid glass of
beer and learn how it arrived in that glass
after only several thousand years

*Old brewery*

*Modern bottling line*

# The
# Beer
# Esthete
# at Home

# The Beer Esthete at Home

Despite the fancy title, this section is not about beer snobbery. It's about beer appreciation. Respecting what you're drinking—and yourself for enjoying it to the fullest extent possible.

To begin with, therefore, whenever you bring home some beer and, if when you taste it, the beer is obviously past its prime, bring it back. The distributor, not the store, has the responsibility for replacing beer that's too old, and the store needs your complaints to ensure its own shelves of beer that's as fresh as possible. Imported beers take considerable time to even reach the retail outlet where you find them, about two-and-a-half months, which in some cases may even be optimistic. So their age is even more at issue, even though they've generally been pasteurized for longer shelf life. Highly hopped imported beers provide some of their own shelf life. There is one rather nifty American brew, Horlacher Brewing's Perfection Beer, which is aged nine months and therefore possesses an unusually long shelf life. But as a rule of thumb I'd say that six months is acceptable, if hardly ideal, and after that you're best advised to remember that beer is a fragile food. Don't buy cases of it and then forget about them. Buy as much as you plan to enjoy. And bottles, rather than cans, please. The only advantages to cans are that they chill faster, and can't break, but these are offset by the possibility of a metallic taste.

Whether you keep beer in the refrigerator, or some cool dark place, keep it upright. It isn't wine. You don't have to keep the cork moist. And beer that's stored on its side suffers far more surface contact with air than when kept upright. Oxygen is the enemy of beer from the moment of storage until the bottle or can is opened. Only then does it help you enjoy the nose of the beer, just as you would begin to appreciate a glass of wine.

# The Beer Esthete at Home

Proper beer temperature is a tricky business for Americans because, just to cite one example, room temperature in a British pub or German *gasthaus* without central heating is not the same as room temperature in the average American home. If you have a basement or cool place, fine, otherwise there are two ways to approach this problem. One is to refrigerate the beers you expect to drink over the next several days and take them out sufficiently ahead so that you taste them, not the chill of your refrigerator. Try fifteen minutes out of the fridge and adjust accordingly for your own taste preferences. The other school of thought is to place beers into the fridge at an appropriate time before you plan to enjoy them. The trouble with both schools of thought is not academic but most practical: an appropriate temperature for lager is not an approppriate temperature for other types of beer—much too cold. What to do? Well, experiment. Lagers really are not best enjoyed below 45 degrees Fahrenheit. Ales and dark beers may taste great to you at 50 degrees, but try them a mite warmer. In fact, try them at room temperature. You may be pleasantly surprised at the new taste nuances you're discovering. Stouts, porters and bocks are definitely in the 55- to 56-degree category. You're dealing with beers sometimes so dense that light won't shine through them, so drinking them really chilled is out of the question. The only thing you're trying to avoid is drinking these malty triumphs of the brewing art too warm. So, again, experiment. It's not much work, but provides enormous satisfaction when you learn how to achieve maximum pleasure with each style of beer.

Another area of multi-faceted theory revolves around pouring. Forget all other theories now. We are going to build the head from the bottom, not the top. Keep the

# The
# Beer
# Esthete
# at Home

glass upright, pour straight down the middle until a respectable head forms. Wait a moment. Let the natural carbonation consolidate itself into a fine head. Then tilt the glass to a 45-degree angle. Pour carefully down the side. You are building the head from underneath instead of competing with it. When the head approaches the top of the glass, bring the glass back to a perpendicular position. Height-of-head theories are really open to debate, but two fingers' worth of foam, including a craggy (indicating natural carbonation) rise above the rim, isn't bad at all.

Glassware is a matter of esthetics, of course, but first let me remind you that beer consumed from any kind of non-transparent mug or stein has *no* visual esthetics. You see the head, but that's about all. By contrast, beer looks swell in elegant glassware. Its color ranges from pale gold to hues darker than any wine to near black; light refraction is most attractive with those having color tones comparable to wine. A more important concern than type of glassware is the top of the glass. Some beer purists prefer the same kind of closed-in glass that helps capture the bubbles from Champagne and other sparkling wines. This would exclude all pilsner glasses in favor of flute glasses, tulip glasses and the French pilsner stemware with the slightly closed tops mentioned earlier. That's the purist's privilege. But I must tell you, a fine-looking beer in a big fat burgundy glass (say, a ten-ouncer) is just fine with me unless I'm at a tasting.

When you're done enjoying your beer, the glasses of course will require washing. Which brings us to a tender subject. To best enjoy beer in those glasses, don't use them for anything else. This may smack of inconvenience or impracticality, but it pays off in drinking pleasure. Glasses used for milk or soft drinks or iced tea, or whatever,

# The
# Beer
# Esthete
# at Home

may leave residues of fat or substances inside the glass, no matter how sincere your dishwasher (human or otherwise). So clean your beer glassware by hand with good old cold water—no soap because it leaves its own residue—and if you choose to dry the glasses, use a lint-free dishtowel. And don't leave the glasses overnight—do them as soon as is convenient after they've been used. If it makes you somehow uneasy to use just cold water, go the standard route but give the glasses a final rinse with cold water to ensure against soap residue.

Since we're kibitzing about enjoying beer at home, I suppose I should tell you about home brewing. But I can't. I can't because I don't do it; I barely got by college chemistry. But if you'll check *Books In Print* at your nearest bookstore, you'll find some titles you may want to investigate. But don't treat home brewing as some kind of game—more than one pantry has been blown away by improperly made or stored beer. A few friends of mine make it, and it's uneven stuff. But when it's good, it's a homemade step back into a gentler time.

# Beer
# in
# the
# Kitchen

# Beer in the Kitchen

No one would claim that beer, considered generically, is preferable to wine with food—in any case, why create a rivalry when both are glorious beverages! Beer is easier to match against the many flavors of Chinese food and also serves as a spice-queller with a variety of fiery cuisines. And beer is never so appreciated as when accompanied by hotdogs and baseball—the great American pastime. Beer also goes well in food, from rich dark stout to light, amber lager. It is not as versatile as wine in this regard, because of its maltiness and hoppy flavor. But it adds gusto and a robust quality to many foods. And it is not without subtleties—consider Beer Sorbet and Sabayon with Blueberries in Hazelnut baskets among the following recipes. As some folks say by way of a funny compliment, this is to die for!

While there are hundreds of recipes calling for beer as a prime ingredient, many of these are variations on a basic theme. We've included a handful of classic recipes, all of which are delicious whether or not you accompany them with a tall lager.

# Beer in the Kitchen

## Cold Beer Soup

1 cup currants
hot water
¾ cup pumpernickel crumbs
1 qt. light beer
½ cup sugar
1 lemon, sliced
1 stick cinnamon
4 cloves
¼ teaspoon nutmeg, grated

Cover currants with hot water and soak 1 hour. Add pumpernickel crumbs and beer, sugar, lemon, cinnamon, cloves and nutmeg. Chill 2 hours in refrigerator. Remove cinnamon, cloves and lemon slices. Stir well and serve with plain crackers or melba toast.
Four servings

## Beer Batter

¾ cup flour
¾ cup light beer, stale and at room temperature
Salt to taste
1 tablespoon melted butter or vegetable oil
1 egg, separated

Put flour in a bowl and stir in beer, salt, and butter or oil. Blend until there are still a few small lumps. Cover bowl and let stand in a warm place 2 or 3 hours. When ready to cook, stir in egg yolk. Beat white until stiff and fold in.
Four to six servings

# Beer in the Kitchen

## Beer Bread

1 envelope granular yeast
2 cups light beer
Salt to taste
4½ cups flour, plus about ½ cup flour for kneading
Oil or lard
1 egg white, lightly beaten
2 tablespoons sesame seeds

Put yeast in a large, warm bowl. Heat beer slowly until lukewarm. Do not overheat. Pour warm beer into bowl and stir until yeast is dissolved. Add salt and stir. Add 4½ cups of flour, kneading. Form into a ball. Turn the ball of dough out onto a floured board and knead for about 10 minutes, until the dough is smooth, soft, and elastic. Grease a large bowl with oil or lard and add the ball of dough. Turn ball to coat all over with grease. Cover with towel and let stand in a warm place until double in bulk, about 2 hours. Turn dough out and knead briefly. Shape into a ball and return to bowl. Cover and let rise until double in bulk, about 45 minutes. Turn the dough out and knead briefly. Divide the dough in half and roll each half out into long sausage. Place the loaves in French bread molds or arrange them on baking sheet sprinkled with cornmeal. Cover with a towel and let rise for 30 minutes. Preheat oven to 400°. Using sharp knife, slash the tops of each loaf with three parallel slashes. Cover again and let rise for 30 minutes longer. Uncover the loaves and brush the tops with egg white. Sprinkle with sesame seeds and place in the oven. Bake for 50 minutes, until browned.
2 loaves

# Beer in the Kitchen

## Vegetable Medley

Beer batter (p.68)
2 zucchini
1 teaspoon salt
1 stalk broccoli
1 small cauliflower
6 radishes
12 greenbeans
12 scallions, white part only
½ cup flour
3 tablespoons Parmesan cheese
Salt to taste
Oil for frying

Prepare batter. Trim and wash zucchini, cut into half-inch slices, and put into colander; sprinkle with salt and let drain for 1 hour. Cut flowers off broccoli, wash them and reserve; peel stalks, cut them into one-inch pieces and parboil for 3 minutes. Cut cauliflower into flowerets, dividing larger ones in two. Trim and wash remaining vegetables and cut in half.

Mix flour, Parmesan cheese, and salt, and dredge all vegetables with mixture. Heat oil in fryer to 375°. Dip vegetable pieces into beer batter and drop into oil; do not fry more than six pieces at a time. When brown on all sides, remove, drain, and keep warm. Serve ungarnished or with capered mayonnaise.

Six servings

# Beer in the Kitchen

## Duck in Beer

5 lb. duck
Salt to taste
½ teaspoon marjoram
1 tablespoon flour
4 tablespoons butter
¾ cup dark beer
¾ cup hot chicken stock
1 clove garlic
1 small onion
1 bay leaf
1 stalk of celery
¼ teaspoon tarragon
2 tablespoons flour mixed with
     3 tablespoons water

Cut duck into serving pieces. Sprinkle with
salt and marjoram and dredge with flour.
Heat butter in skillet with a cover. When hot
add duck and brown well on all sides. Pour
in beer, then add chicken stock. Add garlic,
onion, bay leaf, celery, and tarragon. Cover
and simmer gently about 40 minutes, or until duck is tender. Remove vegetables and
bay leaf. Skim fat from gravy. Stir in flour
diluted in water and simmer, stirring, until
thickened. Put duck on heated serving dish
and pour gravy over it.
Four servings

# Beer in the Kitchen

## Baked Chicken and Apples in Beer

4 lb. chicken, cut into pieces
Salt and pepper to taste
3 tablespoons vegetable oil
1 large onion, slice in rings
4 apples, sliced in rings
1½ tablespoons flour
1½ cups light beer
½ teaspoon thyme
1 tablespoon lemon juice

Preheat oven to 350°. Season chicken pieces with salt and pepper and brown in heated oil. Remove and reserve. Add onion and apple rings to pan and brown over low flame. Cover bottom of greased casserole with half the onion and apple rings, add chicken pieces, and top with remaining onion and apple rings. Stir enough flour into fat remaining in pan to absorb it all. Slowly add beer and cook, stirring constantly, until thickened. Add thyme and lemon juice, pour over chicken mixture in casserole, cover, and bake for 1 hour or until done.
Four to six servings

# Beer
# in
# the
# Kitchen

## Barbecued Spareribs
## with Beer and Honey

6 lbs. spareribs, cut into serving pieces
2 cups light beer
¾ cup honey
1 teaspoon dry mustard
1 tablespoon chili powder
1 teaspoon sage
1 tablespoon salt
2 tablespoons lemon juice

Place ribs in large skillet. Mix the remaining ingredients and pour over the ribs. Let stand in the refrigerator 12 (or more) hours turning several times. Remove the ribs from the marinade, reserving liquid. Place ribs on the rack of a hot charcoal grill or broiler, about four inches from the heat. Cook, turning frequently and brushing with the marinade, about 1½ hours or until ribs are brown and glazed.
Six servings

# Beer in the Kitchen

## Salmon Poached in Beer

4 salmon steaks
2 tablespoons melted butter
¼ cup chopped chives
½ teaspoon salt
1 clove garlic, crushed
2 teaspoons lemon juice
½ cup dark beer
1 teaspoon cornstarch

Soak both parts of a clay pot in water for 15 minutes. Place salmon steaks in pot. Combine the melted butter, parsley, salt, garlic, lemon juice, and beer, and pour over fish. Cover pot and place in a cold oven. Turn oven on to 450°. Cook for 30 minutes. Remove pot from oven and pour off liquid into a saucepan. Return the pot to the oven, without the top, for 5 more minutes, to brown the salmon. Dissolve cornstarch in a little water and add to liquid in saucepan. Heat on low flame, stirring constantly, until thickened. Pour over salmon steaks and serve.
Four servings

# Beer
## in
## the
## Kitchen

### Shrimp Steamed
### in Beer and Dill

1 lb. shrimp
1 bay leaf
8 sprigs fresh dill
1 clove garlic
6 whole peppercorns, crushed
1 teaspoon thyme
⅛ teaspoon Tabasco sauce
1 cup light beer
Salt to taste
2 celery ribs with leaves

Put washed, unpeeled shrimp in saucepan or deep skillet and add remaining ingredients. Cover, bring to a rolling boil, and remove from heat. Serve the shrimp with melted lemon butter.
Two to four servings

# Beer in the Kitchen

## Welsh Rarebit

1 lb. sharp Cheddar, grated
1 tablespoon butter
1 cup lager beer
1 egg
2 teaspoons mustard
2 teaspoons Worchestershire sauce

Heat water in lower part of double boiler and melt the butter in the upper part. Add cheese and stir until it melts. Very slowly blend in beer. Beat egg with mustard and Worchestershire sauce, and add a few spoonfuls of cheese mixture. Then slowly stir the egg mixture into cheese, blending thoroughly. Do not let water boil, and do not overheat cheese mixture. Serve over well-buttered toast.
Four servings

## Kronenbourg Sabayon and Sorbet with Blueberries in Hazelnut Baskets

6 hazelnut baskets
Sorbet
1½ pints blueberries
Sabayon

### HAZELNUT BASKETS

3 egg whites
⅔ cup sugar
4 tablespoons flour
6 tablespoons chopped hazelnuts
⅓ cup butter

Preheat oven to 400°. Beat the egg whites and sugar together until foams. Mix in sifted flour, hazelnuts and butter. Spoon mixture

# Beer in the Kitchen

onto a buttered baking sheet into six circles. Bake for approximately 4 minutes until light brown. Remove from baking sheet with spatula. Mold each to an upside-down cup or bowl. Set aside to cool.

## SORBET

½ lb. granulated sugar
1 cup water
1½ cups Kronenbourg beer
Juice of half an orange
Juice of half a lemon
1 egg white
Crushed ice, coarse salt

Boil water and sugar. Let cool. Mix sugar syrup, beer, orange and lemon juice. Put mixture in three-quart mixing bowl or sauce pan. Set in five-quart mixing bowl or pot filled with crushed ice and coarse salt, using five parts ice to one part salt. Beat syrup-beer mixture until thick (or put mixture through sorbetiere until thick). Keep in freezer unti ready to serve.

## SABAYON

3/8 lbs. sugar
6 egg yolks
3/4 cup Kronenbourg beer

Mix sugar and egg yolks in copper bowl over double boiler until foamy. Add beer and heat over double boiler until thick and creamy. To serve, fill each basket with sorbet. Cover with blueberries. Top with sabayon.
Six servings

*Courtesy of Kronenbourg Brewery

# Beer Around The World

# Beer
# Around
# The
# World

Jägerhaus

Tfhere are more than 1,050 brands of
beer either being imported into or
made in the United States. An impressive number by any reckoning. However, there are more than five thousand
brands of beer in the world—many of them
local or regional brews that don't leave their
areas and a few that don't even leave the
places where they're served. Both in Germany and England, there are made-on-the-
premises beers that are only sold on site.

We can't bring you a "taste" of
those beers, therefore, but we can give you a
taste of the total beer menu around the
world. It's a rather large menu, obviously
enough, so we will concentrate on the nations with the highest beer consumptions
over a considerable period of years—those
where beer has both mystique and international reputation. It might be argued that
the United States does not belong in this
group on either count, but no other nation
produces—and obviously consumes—so
much beer. And an exciting beer culture is
just beginning to brew in America.

The following nations are listed in
the order of their per-capita beer consumption:

# Beer
# Around
# The
# World

## West Germany

Fewer breweries than there used to be, but 900-plus breweries and many styles of beer (5,000 brands) attest to the continuing strength of the German beer *kultur*. Remnants from the past include eleven still-functioning monastical breweries and such place names as Bierstadt, Bieren, Biersdorf, Bierwinkel and Biering. Evidence of the viability of this tradition include the "other Oktoberfest" hosted by Stuttgart, and the annual Kulmbach Beer Week ("The Oktoberfest of Franconia"), which is held each summer. Also, the feisty folk of Cologne and their civil beer-style. In late 1980, an appellate court ruled that only Cologne's twelve breweries may use *Kolsch* (the adjectival spelling of Cologne in German) for their pale, top-fermented beers, which are served in tall, narrow glasses. Six months later, there was a brouhaha in Munich when it was suggested that for security reasons, metal containers be used instead of wooden barrels at the Oktoberfest. To put security-mindedness before tradition didn't sit well with citizens of the world's most famous beer town. Nor did the poll showing Dortmund, the nation's largest beer-producing city, as being perceived as a rival beer capital to Munich. Quantity is not the same as quality, spat back the Muncheners.

In fact, both cities produce estimable beer. Whereas Munich beers are most famous for their malty qualities, Dortmunders provide more balance between hops and maltiness. By contrast, the top-fermented malt styles of Cologne, Dusseldorf and Munster would seem to the American palate Teutonic versions of British ales. The wheat beers of the north and Berlin are now rivaled in the south, but no one matches the potency of Kulmbach beers which undergoes freezing to reach its 13.5 percent alcohol

# Beer Around The World

level. However, various cities' *doppel-bocks*—usually identified by the suffix, "ator," as in Spaten's Optimator and Lowenbrau's Triumphator—are truly lusty beers. And so are the "ordinary" bocks, originally an Einbock northern specialty but now made widely, particularly in Bavaria, in various color shades but all rich, malty and of more than ordinary (minimum of 6 percent) impact. Nor are the *marzenbiers* ("March beers"), the strong festival beers—traditionally drunk (except for sissies) from one-liter mugs—lacking in punch.

In such a cursory examination of the beers from the nation that alone accounts for 75 percent of European Community breweries, numerically speaking, we can but mention the Ostern (Easter) beers and such specialties as Bamberg's *rauchbier,* a smoky brew probably best enjoyed with food. Suffice to say that *bier* has no rivals when it comes to variety and palatability of tastes.

## Belgium

The other nation of so many beer styles. Lager wasn't even produced until the 1890s, but Stella Artois is today the nation's most famous beer, followed by Jupiler although Cristal Alken is said to be the most admired. Belgians guzzle their lagers, but they also practice much local favoritism on behalf of their many other brews: the intense Rodenbach red ales made in West Flanders; brown ales, the almost-black Gildenberg being the product of at least nine months' aging; British-style pale ales; top-fermented Abbey beers, including the five highly prized Trappistes still brewed by Cistercian monks at their abbeys, as well as less heavenly Trappist beers licensed to commercial brewers; dark "strong ales" that

# Beer Around The World

.he name with 8 percent alcohol; ...s, summer ales favored by Walloons; ...diosyncratic ales that are truly Belgian ...haracter, the best example being Ant- ...p's popular De Koninck. In addition to ...tom-fermented "white" wheat beers—so ...led because of their cloudy color- ...g—there are the spontaneously fermented ...*imbic* beers utilizing free-floating wild *yeasts* instead of brewer's yeasts. In a concession to the brewer's art, a blend of wheat and barley is used. But there tradition ends: These beers are consumed "young" (cloudy and very bitter-sour) at three months' and "old" (not less than two but more likely three-four) when they're clearer and bittersweet. Far more often, they're used for *gueuze* beers, blends of old-young lambics that go through a secondary Champagne-type fermentation in the bottle and are best enjoyed two years after bottling. Other variants of lambics: *kriek,* sweetened with whole cherries steeped in the beer for four-to-eight months, and *faro,* a blend of high and medium density lambics slightly sweetened with sugar candy. Belgium also has three beer museums, its own *Oktoberfeesten* (in Flanders' Wieze) plus many other festivals, and beer bottles (these fruity lambic types) that are really Champagne and Burgundy bottles. Somehow, it all makes sense.

## Czechoslovakia

Rival to Belgium as second-biggest per capita consumer over the years, this nation entertained no international rivalry, among pilsners, to its Pilsner Urquell. Within the nation, though, there are fierce partisans for several Prague pilsners as well as those from other areas, most especially Budvar, made in the southwestern region. (Its German name, Budweis, may sound fa-

# Beer
# Around
# The
# World

miliar to Americans because Adolphus
Busch borrowed it for his St. Louis brew.)
There are also very decent beers with less
body weight than pilsners, both dark and
light varieties, and some with sweetish tastes
belying the strong presence of Czech hops.
They're known as "draft (draught) beers,"
even though some are only sold bottled.
There are also dark, malty beers, sometimes
in the Munich style but of a considerable
variety, including porters made in the East
Bohemia and Central Slovak regions. Unlike Germany, Czechoslovakia has two more
or less national beers, Pilsner Urquell and
Budvar, but the same delicious regionalism
is present here as in Belgium.

## Australia

In Darwin, the beer-consuming
capital of the nation, the yearly per-capita
beer consumption is a rollicking sixty gal-
lons per adult. Other northern territory resi-
dents may even do a little better. But spoil-
sports elsewhere bring Australia's per-capita
statistics down quite a lot. Although beer remains an essentially male religion here, there
are tempering influences trying to persuade
the macho types that beer doesn't have to be
served so cold, or knocked back so fast, so
as not to. . . get paralyzed. Australia, despite
its ancestry, specializes in lagers—because of
the climate—but they're strong, hoppy
beers that haven't gotten the ale taste out of
their brewing systems. And the ales, with a
definite English accent, can be world-class
brews. By reputation Foster's, made by the
giant Carlton & United Brewer brewing
combine, and Swan, Toohey and Tooth are
the famous beer names—generally on merit,
I might add—but the ales and stouts produced by Castlemaine Perkins Ltd. and
Cooper & Sons deserve more appreciation

# Beer Around The World

outside Australia. Indeed, the British, who can be patronizing toward things Australian, should be grateful that their brewing traditions are being honored, to very good effect, in this former colony.

## New Zealand

Not just a branch of Australia, this lusty beer-drinking nation saw the temperance movement help force its brewing industry into just three "groups" and many fewer brands than in yesteryear. Leopard and Lion are the top-selling brands, but Steinlager, a classy, zesty lager, is preferred by many with sophisticated palates. They're right—this is a world-class brew.

## Luxembourg

Tiny nation, very prosperous and big drinkers. Six brewers for 650,000 people, light to dark beers. I've not had the beers of Brasseries Simon, locally well-regarded, but have tasted Diekirch's both in and out of the country, and find the pilsner a grand beer, more than befitting this Grand Dutchy.

## Denmark

It used to be Carlsberg and Tuborg, Tuborg and Carlsberg. They even became one company—United Breweries. This may not have been such a great idea. In America, the Tuborg has been licensed to a major American brewer, Miller, to its detriment as a world-class beer. The export of Carlsberg, brewed under license in Canada, lacks the flavor and character of the Danish-made brand. This may reflect what is perceived as the American taste, and if so, it's a

# Beer Around The World

mistake—Americans have been attracted to imported beers precisely because they have *more* taste. In any case, my last visit to Denmark found both Carlsberg and Tuborg producing a dozen-plus superior brands for domestic consumption. Rivaling them, on a local basis, are the products of Ceres and Albani breweries—happily, its excellent porter is exported to America—those of Elsinore's Wiibroe Brewery. I'm sad to report, if only for literary reasons, that its Hamlet and Ophelia brand has been dethroned by Nanook of the North. On the other hand, appreciation should be expressed for such heroic-sounding breweries as Neptun, Odin and Thor. Lolland-Falsters exports a decent lager to America, but the firm deserves more praise for its charming labels featuring both happy-looking humans and properly ferocious wild animals. The very likable Danes manage to have breweries that reflecting the national character.

## Ireland

Guinness is not the only drinking game in town. Cork has Murphy's, a fine stout, and other locals offer Beamish & Crawford, another staunch stout. But Dublin is County Guinness country, and this dark, creamy, lusty, and fullsome unpasteurized brew symbolizes Ireland as no other beer does its particular nation. Oh, there's Harp lager, a Guinness property, and Macardle's Phoenix and Smithwick's ales. These represent decent drink and are all owned or controlled by Guinness. They are said to be gaining in popularity, particularly among the young, often inclined to prefer something other than the drink of their elders. But they aren't Ireland. No, Ireland is watching a publican "building a proper pint" of stout, an artisan raising the

# Beer Around The World

craft of bartending to another level. There's a lot of mystique in that tall pint glass, plus twenty ounces of brewing also rendered into art form. Hyperbole? Perhaps. But that's the Irish way, too, and if you're "not likin' it," as they say, you doubtless won't enjoy drinking in the company of leprechauns.

## Great Britain

If nothing else, the Campaign for Real Ale has resulted in one very respectable real ale from the major brewers, Courage's Directors. However, the real import of the movement—apart from saying a loud "No" to the homogenizing trends of the giant brewers—has been to arrest some of the drastic shrinkage of Britain's brewing industry. There were 16,000 brewers a century ago, 3,000 a decade ago, and there are half that number today. This has been accomplished by bringing attention to the excellent choices remaining—some 300 real ales that are the best examples of the glorious beers of yesteryear. Not a bland, fizzy beer in the lot, real ale is defined as "beer brewed from malted barley and hops, stored in barrels, and served by methods which do not use carbon dioxide pressure. . . . It should leave the brewery in its natural state—still able to ferment in the cask. It should not be filtered or pasteurized, for both processes take the body out of the beer. . . . Real ale must be stored in barrels or casks which have two holes—one to let the beer out and one to let the air in, so that the beer can breathe and continue to ferment."

From the point of view of the national brewers, there were a series of production nightmares involved in old-time brewing methods, as well as potential problems at the pub itself. Unfiltered and unpasteurized beers require great care and at-

# Beer Around The World

tention, must be kept at the right temperature and should be consumed within an appropriate period of time to avoid spoilage. So the big brewers had some reasonable motives when they introduced keg beers. But they tried to sell it as something better, and worse yet, the trendy new drink. The same sort of thinking went into the "tarting up" of many pubs, giving them cutesy themes—nautical, wild west, you-name-it—or turning them into discos, or both. Esthetics aside, there were sound economic reasons for this development. Television had lured many families away from the pubs; young people weren't patronizing them—they weren't "fun places"; and only those devoted to their "local" were on hand. Still, if you were a regular and suddenly saw your pub turned into something not remotely British and populated by gyrating youngsters, you'd wonder about the large brewers' ingratitude for your loyal patronage over the years. The problem was undeniably complex, and CAMRA addressed itself to it not by insisting that keg beers, with inferior ingredients and $CO_2$, just bubble away, but by insisting that a wide range of choice be encouraged. Nor could the shabbiness of many old pubs be ignored. CAMRA, according to Michael Hardman, a founding-member, "is also concerned with pubs as well as beer. Too many pubs are ugly drinking-troughs, decorated in appalling taste. We're concerned about pub food and pub games as well, and we also want changes made in our ludicrous licensing system."

Ultimately the real arbitors are the beer drinkers, most of whom fancy themselves experts on their pint. They're used to choice—bitter, best bitter on draft, in bottles, pale ale, export ale, brown ale, stout and lager, plus barley wine for connoisseurs and heroes. And now they've got more beers

# Beer
# Around
# The
# World

from which to choose because of regional beers coming to the "free houses" of the major cities. Progress includes preserving the best of the past, and then building on that foundation, doesn't it? Well, if so, the "good guys" have won the most recent Battle of Britain.

## Austria

Vienna used to be a great brewing center, and its amber lagers were a beer-style unto themselves. This tradition survives in the form of *spezial* beers, but the predominant style is that of German-type lagers. Bocks, of varying color-tones are also produced. To a visitor, Austria (particularly Vienna) has seemed to be trapped in the past, having bet on the wrong side in two world wars. Yet there is joy, or else nostalgic self-indulgence, taken in what remains of Austria's once proud brewing tradition. Vienna is not fabled for its beer halls, but Salzburg and Graz are. And of the principal brands exported, Gooser and Puntigam can hold up their heads among the world's beers.

On the local level, there are a few dozen breweries selling traditional, unpasteurized beers. Thus, while the glory may be gone, some very respectable brews remain to honor the past.

## Canada

To an American who has spent some time in Canada, the popularity of a few Canadian brews is oddly irksome because they provide more taste than most American beers but don't adequately represent the real range and excellence of Canadian beer. A kind of reverse snobbery is going on here: They're catering to American taste by just allowing us a taste of their taste. On the other hand, this doesn't mean to say that I'm not grateful for Moosehead and products of the "Big Three" of Canadian brewing—Carling O'Keefe, Labatt's and Molson—reaching across the border. But nationally we're receiving easily three times as many German beers as we are from our neighbors to the north. For example, Uncle Ben is no longer with his brewery—Ben Ginter, a 240-pound ex-bulldozer operator ("cat skinner") who became one of Canada's biggest independent brewers, then ran into money problems in 1976. But the new owners continue to make Pacific Gold Beer and Yukon Gold Premium Pilsner, two brands American beer-lovers would surely like. Then, too, Canadians prefer lager to ale, but ales are still readily available, unlike in America. As an ale-man myself, I wouldn't mind having access to Carling O'Keefe's Red Cap Ale. Labatt's 50 Ale, available here, is Canada's top-selling ale, but I'd like to retaste the firm's India Pale and Extra Stock Ales. Oland's Brewery, part of the giant Labatt's complex stretching across Canada, produces beers well-regarded on Nova Scotia, New Brunswick and Newfoundland, among them Old Scotia Ale and Extra Stout. Another Labatt's property, Alexander Keith's Nova Scotia Brewery, produces its own admirable version of IPA (India Pale Ale). Moosehead Special Ale and Molson Porter are two other products that should appeal to Americans who like a lot of hoppiness and maltiness, respectively, in their beer. So too with Dow Cream Porter, especially since this type of malty beer is so rare in the United States.

Whether all these products will actually be exported, of course, depends on the state of brewing in Canada itself. The big guys are absorbing the little guys, as usual,

# Beer
# Around
# The
# World

although some continue to operate under the corporate umbrella—and Americans respond to the fuller-bodied, stronger (usually 5 percent) Canadian brews. Their ales, for example, do well in the East, but what about the Sun Belt? Or, why drink the Henninger German-style beers since so many German exports are already here? Answer: They're pretty good and they cost less!

Of course one can always visit Canada to taste its beers, but be prepared for a well-defined obstacle course of blue laws, that nation's hangover from its regional experiments with Prohibition. In many places a man thirsting for a beer on Sunday will either have to emigrate south or wait until Monday. And if you want to buy alcoholic beverages in an atmosphere totally devoid of interest, much less charm, try the government liquor stores. You'll have to do just that, in terms of retail sales, in most places because other outlets don't exist. Canada, it seems, produces some excellent alcoholic beverages (excluding its champagne), but doesn't want too many Canadians enjoying them.

## United States

Ostensibly the real beer news in America is always business rather than consumer oriented. Seventh-ranked Stroh Brewery took over tenth-ranked F & M Schaefer in the spring of 1981 and hoped its Detroit beer, a favorite of autoworkers, would assume some cult status in the East as it had on some campuses. Bud and Miller continue to duke it out, with Anheuser-Bush (over 28 percent of the market) bringing out Natural Light to challenge Miller's well-advertised product. Is this big news? Not to me. It isn't news after I realized that Michelob Light tasted pretty good

# Beer
# Around
# The
# World

because it had only a few less calories than the regular Michelob, which itself may not be as good as it used to be but now ranks No. 7 among domestic beers, despite its super-premium price.

Still, Miller Lite got the Philip Morris subsidiary ahead of Schlitz in the beer sweepstakes—with some masochistic assists from Schlitz, which had to reformulate its product because of sagging sales. And now Miller has a malt liquor called Magnum to compete with Schlitz' popular malt liquor Bull. Schlitz was No. 1 once, but now Miller and Anheuser-Busch own nearly half the market. That's rough competition. Yet regional beers can still do very well. Witness Stroh, seventh-ranked brand in the nation. And G. Heileman, fastest-growing (through acquisition) U.S. brewer, with around forty brands but none of them national.

I don't want you to think that none of this is interesting stuff—no writer can write about the product and not be informed on the industry producing it. But if you're at all romantic about beer, you'll want to know about the little guys—a few very little indeed—and their products. What about Henry Weinhard's Private Reserve Beer, made by the Portland, Oregon, firm of Blitz-Weinhard (a Pabst subsidiary)? It's selling well out there, but taste reports are less inspired. Beer lovers of Milwaukee, Wisconsin, swear by Point and Leinenkugel. I find the former pretty good, not great, but haven't been able to get close to the latter. And it is important, perhaps essential, to taste these beers fairly close to their homes. Utica, N.Y., is the home of Maximus Super Beer, a local jewel, Genesee Bock, made in Rochester, N.Y., another. In Pennsylvania, aside from previously mentioned beers, Erie boasts a kind of unique item, Koehler, an American brew said to have a Dutch accent, and Latrobe, one of the few U.S. breweries named after their towns, has gained out-of-state status for its Rolling Rock Premium Beer. By contrast, you have to go to St. Mary's, Pa., to be sure of Straub, for this admirable little brewery doesn't advertise or promote, just makes a beer relished by locals and envied by others. Another example of fermentation envy: Jax, much admired in New Orleans, is the pearl of San Antonio, Texas, hundreds of miles away.

Pearl Brewing, makers of Jax, is hardly a small brewery. However, Spoetz in Shiner, Texas, is very tiny and no one I know has ever tasted its beer. And, like Straub, not trying to grow. By marked contrast, Anchor Brewing in San Francisco has gained wide attention for its top-flight Anchor Steam Beer and Porter brands. Steam beer, perhaps the only truly indigeneous American beer, originated back in the Gold Rush days. Demand for beer was high, supplies of ice low. Although bottom-fermented, the beers were brewed at a higher temperature (no ice for cooling) than usual for lagers and came out as a combination ale-lager. When it came out literally, the pressure released from the cask was dubbed "steam." Those beers also had a head of robust foam. Today's Anchor Steam is probably better than any of those old-time brews, because of quality control; its popularity has allowed the tiny firm to double its brewing capacities.

Probably because of Anchor's success, a boutique brewery has sprung up in San Rafael, California—Steam Beer Brewing. And California, which sets many a trend has other boutique breweries: New Albion (the first), Thomas Arthur De Bakker, Mendenhall, Ozeki San Benito and the oddly named Berkeley concern, Numano Sake Co. (Sake is a rice wine before becoming a beer, so maybe that explains it). But Califor-

# Beer Around The World

nia has no exclusive on this new phenomenon—boutique breweries are in New York, Colorado and elsewhere.

Will this new brewing activity make a difference? Well, certainly not nationally, but imports are projected by some industry observers at 15 percent of the total U.S. market. And Coors, Heileman, Olympia and Schlitz haven't been test-marketing super-premium brands because the economy is so wonderful. No, Americans are increasingly buying the better beers—as they perceive them—and this, taken with the ever-increasing consumption patterns over more than two-decades, bodes well for American beer. The brewers have gone the light, homogenized route and have found its newest incarnation-low-cal beers very successful. But to meet this new demand for more taste and different tastes, they need but look to what American brews used to taste like before Prohibition. Lots and lots of good brews then. So Americans don't have dumb tastebuds. And they like beer a lot—they drink a daily 8-ounce serving per citizen, and while that doesn't rank them anywhere near the world leaders, it only translates into another 4-ounces a day to be one of the world's leaders. The seventies were the decade of wine discovery in America. The eighties, it seems to me, will be America's New Age of Beer. A happy, well-hopped thought....

## Holland

Heineken sent America a beer so pleasing that it alone came to represent over 45 percent of the import market during part of the late 1970s. The current export version I've recently tasted reminds me not of Amsterdam, Rotterdam or Hertogenbosch but more of Milwaukee or St. Louis. A big mistake, this, to pander to standard American taste—what made the beer so attractive were its crisp, assertive, flavorful qualities, the same enjoyed overseas. Similarly, the estimable Amstel is available here only in its Light version. Heineken owns Amstel. I now drink Grolsch instead. And hard-to-find Oranjeboom, owned by the Skol (Anglo-Dutch) interests. In Holland, I'd pay homage to all four of these brands, plus some of the fine regional ones, if they haven't been amalgamated away. But unlike the Dutch, I prefer my beer straight—not to wash down a Dutch liqueur. The practice is fun, the headache horrendous.

## France

The French don't rave about their beer as they do their wines, but that is slowly changing. The top-fermented beers of Region du Nord and the lagers of Lorraine and Alsace, splitting that region thought of as a single entity, are either improving or else Frenchmen are belatedly recognizing their worth. French beer is no longer merely Kronenbourg, Europe's most popular bottled beer. There are equally distinguished beers. As for the marketplace, in the northern regions beer seems to appeal to everyone, but elsewhere it's the youth who are making sales and production really spurt ahead. (And who was it that said kids have no taste!)

## Japan

Kirin is either the world's second or third most popular beer. Yet Kirin, part of the truly awesome Mitsubishi conglomerate, is hardly without competition, thanks to

# Beer Around The World

Japanese laws. Sapporo, Asahi and Suntory are the major rival brewers. Suntory, as it happens, is only the world's largest producer of alcoholic goods. Its is very aggressive in promoting Japan's version of Scotch. Yet at home all its beer is unpasteurized, the same as much of Sapporo's and Asahi's output. There may be more really decent beers being served on draft in Japan than in America.

## Mexico

Probably brand for brand, at one point a few decades ago, the best beer country in the Northern hemisphere. German traditions, crisp, refreshing lagers, increasingly assertive dark beers. Not a terribly wide range, but not an unpleasant beer in the lot. Unfortunately, the Mexicans seem to have picked up the "light" mind-swaggle of their neighbors to the north and gave some of their beer more of a U.S. than German inflection. In a much-publicized New West beer-tasting test, however, four Mexican imports ranked among the top eight in a limited selection. And since I'm not going to rank Tecate among my preferred brands, I'd like to confess this: I'm not crazy about teqila, but I will readily consume a can of Tecate, lime juice sprinkled around the top of the can—Tecate is only available in cans—coarse salt near the opening. Unless otherwise forced to do so, I would not drink any other beer in the world directly from the can.